SMARTYpants
secrets

SOCIAL SKILLS

The Top 10 Most Important to Possess

D.R. Martin, PhD*

(*Personal human Development)

Smarty Pants Press
Falmouth, Maine 04105
www.SmartyPantssecrets.com

ISBN 13: 978-1-943971-18-3
ISBN 10: 1943971188

Copyright 2016 D.R. Martin, PhD*
(*Personal human Development)

Disclaimer: This is an informational guide and is not intended as a substitute for legal or other professional services. Readers are urged to consult a variety of sources and educate themselves more fully about the designated topic. While every effort has been made to make this guide accurate, it may contain typographical and content errors. The information expressed herein is the sole researched and experienced opinion of the author(s), is not intended to reflect upon any particular person or company. The author(s) and publisher shall have no responsibility or liability with respect to any loss or damage caused, or alleged to be caused, by the information or application contained in this guide.

The SmartyPants Secrets Concept

A **SmartyPants Secret** is that **one piece of information** that you need to know to make every job a little bit, or maybe a lot, **easier**. Almost everything we do in life has a SmartyPants secret that to it, that knowing the "secret" would help tremendously in shortening the learning curve.

After experiencing many "a ha!" moments that were previous head bangers, I realized that there was a lot of grief – i.e. aggravation, wasted time, spent resources - that could have been saved if I had known to tap into the insider information that others had and I was lacking. A SmartyPants secret is that crucial bit of timely knowledge.

We all want a magic bullet answer that solves all of our problems in one fell swoop and makes everything go perfectly well, preferably in record time! We want that magic to happen right NOW, to be easily done, and to be preferably cheap, or at least not at great expense. There are a lot of demands on our unattainable magic ☺

For example, one day I looked at my face and damn if I didn't see a "sun spot" (nastily also called a "liver" spot) marring the surface of my otherwise smooth face on the right lower cheek. I scheduled an appointment at the dermatologist to verify the find and see if it could be lasered off. She sent me to an aesthetician who gave me some key information that made a huge difference in my decision of what to do next.

I was told that my even slightly darker (Asian) skin carries more pigment than Caucasian skin obviously. But what's not obvious is the way the body works, specifically the way the skin works, which is that when you wound the skin's surface, which laser surgery would certainly do, extra pigments rush to the spot to heal it (the "job" of pigment is to protect the underlying cells). The net result is that non-Caucasian skin heals into darker scabs and scars. (I have noticed this phenomena before but never made a direct connection.) Why then would I ever choose to have laser surgery on my face to remove a mark only to end up with an even darker mark? Yikes!

Obviously I wouldn't, but without this specialized knowledge about different results with different skin types, that even the dermatologist didn't know (yes, she was the recommender of the laser surgery option) I would've made a poor decision, with permanent negative results. A SmartyPants timely secret to the rescue!

Experts, who have hours of experience doing what the newbie is attempting to do, have expert knowledge, which may not be so secret, but it is **key information** that the novice greatly needs.

If you've ever struggled with something then learned the 'something' afterwards that caused you to say to yourself or to say aloud, "*Well, if I only known THAT before I did this*, *it would've made a world of difference!*" then you just learned a SmartyPants secret - the hard way.

The short SmartyPants Secrets books give you the secret that you need on a given topic, the most important piece of information that makes the greatest difference between easier success and hard-fought failure.

When I was young there was a professor at Cornell University, which in his obituary listed him as "*the last man to know everything*." I was taken by the concept of anyone knowing everything there is to know contained in one brain. Oh, to have such a mind!

But **to know everything**, logical facts and figures, and **to be able to do everything** are **two different things**. Brain power doesn't equal skill and expertise.

Today that one brain that knows everything is the Internet. There is so much information today available on the Internet; we can all be like that professor at Cornell and have access to all knowledge at the click of our fingertips.

More knowledge than we could ever consume - **who has time** to go through it all? Most of the time **what you really want is to know is the crux of the subject** on hand, not the whole litany of everything imaginable that is available to know.

Tell me just what I need to know! (and I likely don't know what specific knowledge to ask for). It's literally impossible to know what you don't know. Let the expertise of knowledgeable others guide you.

If you are new to a topic the **SmartyPants secret can save you time and effort**, which are important to your success. Not a complete course on the topic, which you can certainly get elsewhere, the SmartyPants secrets concept is primarily to help you **not miss the key information needed for success**.

The building block of knowledge that the foundation rests upon; the Keystone or cornerstone knowledge makes a critical difference, especially when that knowledge that you do have, or think you have, is **faulty, incomplete or missing** entirely.

The concept of **social proof** states that when we have no prior experience in a given situation we rely on **others to show us the way**. We believe that lacking personal knowledge, that their situation is similar to our situation, and therefore what worked for them has a high probability of working for us.

We quiz others about our shared circumstances around the situation to verify that their solution is a good one. Plus, we think: *there's nothing to lose in trying since I don't have a better answer.*

Then when what worked for another doesn't happen to work for us, we are reminded that **we are all different people**, with different variables that impact success or failure. Some solutions to problems are hit or miss depending on who we are. And sometimes success depends on having and following the right key knowledge.

Solving problems is not the complete SmartyPants concept, although SmartyPants secrets can indeed offer real help for real problems. Rather the full concept is that having that key knowledge piece makes efforts easier and successful quicker; hopefully **avoiding having the problem in the first place**. We do anything in life because we have a goal to achieve. Reaching that goal successfully, quickly and easier than without knowing the SmartPants secret is the SmartyPants concept.

And because **all SmartyPants secrets have a physiological root**, grounded in our shared human biology, every SmartyPants secret is valid for everyone, no matter who you are. While we are all uniquely different from each other, we have a **common biology** consisting of inherited traits that stretch back to the Neanderthal era.

Applying a SmartyPants secret **will work for you no matter who you are**. And in our busy world, who doesn't want to save time and know the SmartyPants secret to anything?

Why ever risk hindering easier success by not knowing the core success secret?

SOCIAL SKILLS

WHY Bother? Why Care?

Because we do care, that's why! We are actually hard-wired to want to be liked, to want to be valued by others, to want others' respect and to feel important.

We are lucky to be here! There is a 1 in a billion sperm chance that YOU are born – so we want to make the most of this opportunity while we are here.

Relationships are the fabric of an enjoyable life. We need healthy relationships with others for us to thrive – our happiness depends on having decent to great social skills. Let's get to it!

SOME PEOPLE ARE JUST...

Unlucky...? (and grew up to be socially awkward) ... Not confident enough...

Overly, painfully SHY (beyond introverted)...

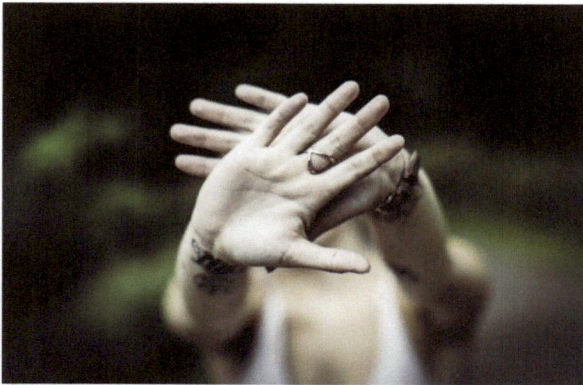

Maybe you think you were shortchanged in the charm department. What comes easy to some may be oh so hard for you. Striking up a conversation with others – why do so, you wonder... what's the point? Making small talk at a social event – abhorrent. When the lack of social skills, or aversion to using them interferes with life's forward movement in a pleasurable way, when you wish you weren't quite so reticent because it's hurting your sociability and making you lonely, that's when it's time to make a conscious change. Social skills can be learned.

Glad-handing politicians and salespeople, everyone knows they just want something from you, and you need to resist getting sucked in to their charisma - or you risk losing your shirt, right? All the Chatty Cathys of the world need to just button it, agreed?! These extreme types are on the opposite end of the social skills spectrum and not the aim here. Manipulators, conversation hogs, pompous boasters wield their dubious communication skills like a weapon and are indeed a social danger to avoid.

Instead, let's focus on developing authentic skills to help life's interactions with others be more enjoyable.

KEY: Develop a style that invites others to be comfortable associating with you

The 10 Top Social Skills List

Social Skill #1: BE POSITIVE

- *Smile!* A lot, if you can. Smile when you see others in greeting. Smile to yourself when you think of something pleasant. Smile when no one is looking – doing so lifts your mood and makes you more productive. Smile when you catch someone's eye, known or unknown to you. Just smile as a new way of being, which reflects in a brighter, positive attitude.

Don't plaster on a big fake smile that says 'forced, disingenuous'. And not a little snide smile that hints at condescension, ugh! I had a boss who walked around the office all day with a similar smile on her face that I wanted to tell her to wipe off; it started to look like a sneer, which is never good.

Smile by just pulling up the corners of your mouth, which rise slowly as the genuine emotion develops, eventually reaching your eyes. This is a real smile, not full-on beaming from ear to ear (reserved for special people and special occasions), but still genuine from the heart, every day.

The corners of the mouth naturally pull down with gravity and age, which makes a face at rest look grumpy. Train your mouth corners to rest slightly up, which will have a dramatic effect on how others perceive you :)

- Maintain an upbeat outlook. Have an attitude that consistently looks on the bright side. Sure things go wrong and life is not always a bed of roses, but reframe the negative as positive, since everything has a bright side. You just need to look for it.

The difference between a consistently optimistic view and a consistently pessimistic view is measurable in successful outcomes. Train yourself to see the glass as half full, not as half empty. If it's Wednesday of vacation week, do you think, "It seems like the vacation just started and now it's already half over!" Or do you instead reframe to: "4 more full vacation days still left to enjoy!"

- *Be witty!* Make others laugh (not necessarily with jokes) with self-deprecating humor and a witty observational take on the world. Laugh with me not at me (and not at others, which is just mean and not endearing).

Humor, smiling and laughing releases endorphins, the body's feel good hormone. We get a natural high from laughing, which is why we like to do it so much, and like people who make us laugh. Humor is the top trait that women look for in a perspective date.

But few of us are professional comedians, so jokes are to be avoided unless the delivery is spot on. Wit is the way to go. A clever turn of a phrase. An inspired use of language that turns a bad situation into a smile. A wry comment on our human foibles that all can relate to is bonding.

- *Reframe negatives* into positives

Small negatives, big negatives – all have some positive aspect. I walk upstairs and forget to take an item I meant to bring, necessitating another trip upstairs (small negative) – reframed to: 'I'm glad to have the opportunity to get more needed exercise.' Big negative – I drive the 2 hours home from visiting relatives only to realize when pulling into my driveway that I left my purse/cell phone behind, necessitating a turn around trip to retrieve it. Reframe to: 'Gives me more time to listen to that audio book' or 'Gives me another visit with the relatives' or 'Gives me a lesson on putting a system in place so I don't forget and do this again' – there's always a positive to reframe to.

The reframing is done internally with self-talk, with an external result of positive enthusiasm. And enthusiasm is contagious. Others like being around positive, energetic, fun people. We hope by being around them that some of it will rub off on us :)

Contrast that to the sad, glum, in the doldrums person who no one wants to be around.

This social skill - to smile and genuinely have an optimistic outlook – comes naturally to some, not as naturally to others. For those in the latter category, it maybe an effort to develop this trait, but it's well worth doing for the social dividends it will pay in the long run.

Social Skill #2: SHOW CONFIDENCE

- Take advantage of the Power Pose
The mind and body are tightly linked on so many levels. The mind controls much of bodily functions but it's also a 2-way exchange: when the body is in a response position, the mind flows. The mind-body connection is very powerful and when known, extremely useful to deliver a confident mind from a pose of confidence (held for a full minute or more).

With the confidence pose – hands raised or on hips, feet spread and firmly planted, head held high, back straight – the body tells the mind it is confident, and the mind follows suit. The confidence becomes real.

- Be assertive and direct; assertiveness, not arrogrance, screams confidence. No one likes arrogance, that in-your-face get-out-of-my-way brashness that saids I'm better than you and you don't count. We all want to feel valued, like we matter. Assertiveness says just that – I matter and you're not going to push me aside or ignore my rights. Assertiveness = confidence, and is very appealing.

- Talk to everyone, be out-of-your-way friendly, be helpful, have genuine concern for others. What you give socially to others is repaid back to you tenfold in social goodwill and capital. But it must be given with pure intentions, not to set up a future quid pro quo debt. Do it because you really care for others and their feelings, and they will care for you in return.

- Stand tall with good posture. Take up space naturally, a top sign of confidence. When you are comfortable in your own skin and move through time and space in an expansive way, others are drawn to that confidence that is neither reticent nor abrasive.

Everybody loves a confident person; not a boisterous, arrogant, overbearing know-it-all. Confidence doesn't require being loud or in-your-face, but rather the opposite, always in possession of a serenity that confidence brings.

A confident person easily gains respect and owns that elusive quality called 'presence'.

*Confidence can be learned – how to gain it, how to maintain it, how to deliver it for yourself on just those tense situations when you need it the most.

*Learn more about this topic in the *SmartyPants Secrets Confidence* book, an entire book devoted to this subject, found on the website at www.SmartyPantsSecrets.com or on Amazon books.

Social Skill #3: THE POWER OF TOUCH

- We crave connection, intimacy, socializing with others - some with a lot of others, some with just a few others, but all need connection with others not just to survive, but to thrive.

- In a literal sense we need others, as we can't get by in this world as totally solitary creatures. So cooperation, socialization, and connection are ingrained traits in all people.

- Touch is very powerful, therefore it must be used wisely and carefully – don't overuse it, be respectful of boundaries – or it will be to your detriment. But do use touch very intentionally.

- Handshakes, hugs, a light tap on an acceptable 'public' body part – even very brief in duration, has enormous subconscious impact on likability, rapport building, and bonding.

- When touch is absent, it may not be consciously noticed as being missing, but the social interaction will definitely suffer because of the lack. This can be remedied by using an understanding the real power of touch to bring people together.

Social Skill #4: CONVERSING - WHAT TO TALK ABOUT

- Talk about IDEAS, not about people

- Talk positively about others, not talking solely about yourself and your experiences; *be interested over being interesting*

- Tell stories. Have some (3) prepared stories that illustrate a positive trait, a humorous lesson learned, a meaningful connection with a respected mentor.
Stories are memorable, especially when they contain vivid specific details that bring them to life. Make yours good enough to be repeated!

- Actively listen. Ask probing, open-ended questions that require more than a yes or no answer. Well constructed questions help people to open up and formulate their thoughts around answering well.

People love to talk about themselves, but it requires a good listener on the other end of the conversation. Being that good listener is a tremendous social skill to possess, and will make you wildly popular.

- Draw meaningful connections between your life and the other person's life. Common experiences and values are great conversation starters.

We like others who are like us. Those commonalities that we share draw us in and bind us to others who are like us. We truly enjoy their company, because they are so much a reflection of our own. Ever met someone of whom you thought or said, 'We've only just met, but it feels like I've known you for years'? That's because they remind you so much of yourself, who you have known for years! Be that person who invokes that known-you-for-years feeling in others by putting the other person so much at ease with your similarities.

A connection can be made meaningful when you raise it above the mundane and give it a specialness. We may be from the same state, or even from the same hometown, that's trivial to some people as there are millions of people in the state. But when you go beyond simply the state's name and relate the commonality to childhood experiences, growing up with all that entails, now that home state commonality is elevated to so much more.

Get chatting! – the more you practice the skill of conversing, the better you will get at it.

Social Skill #5: BE RELIABLE

- Be dependable, be good for your word. When you say you'll deliver, deliver consistently on your promises.

One thing that is universally disliked in society is someone who goes against their word, a welcher, a cheater, who fails to pay his debt. Their word is meaningless; make yours the gold standard.

- Speak up, commit to supporting a person or a good cause, then over-deliver where possible. Go above and beyond, giving 110% effort.

- Be known as someone who can really be counted on to come through routinely, not just occasionally. Be the go-to person others call on in a pinch.

Social Skill #6: BE HUMBLE

- Put your ego aside. Learn something from everyone; every experience teaches you something new, if you're open to receiving it.

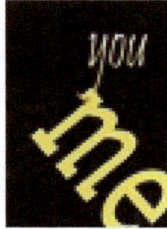

- Be honest, authentic, and truthful

- Be nice, considerate, polite, respectful, tactful

- Don't be a wallflower, but don't overly tooting your own horn either. Be gracious when compliments come your way for achievements and honors, and you will be respected and admired for your truly humble demeanor.

Social Skill #7: BE WELL-GROOMED

Cleanliness and grooming count – a lot.
Impressions are quickly made, which stick for a long time. Plus there is a strong belief that a person's exterior is an accurate reflection of their internal character.

- Find a style that is modern, modest, and complimentary - re: dress attire, re: hairstyle, re: accessories (the little details all add up to the bigger picture).

- Well groomed people are confident people, and they are given more latitude. When something negative happens, they are given the advantage of the benefit of the doubt, whether warranted or not.

Good grooming is well within everybody's control, but is often taken for granted as less important than it really is. The assumption is that personal comfort is more important than respect for the other person, which comes across in our chosen public appearance.

Like other habits, good grooming can easily be made habitual. Once developed, it becomes automatic and we don't have to think about applying this skill, that can easily turn into just another good habit

Another distinct advantage, other than the social advantages that good grooming allows when others treat us with more respect, is the internal advantage of feeling better about ourselves when we are well groomed.

Grooming is a matter of pride and should be consistently maintained, developing a solid positive image whenever we are out in public.

Social Skill #8: ADDRESS THE PERSON BY NAME

- Use their name – a favorite word for everyone - but don't overuse it

- First name? Or Mr/Ms Last Name?
What you have permission to use?
Don't assume an over-friendly position of intimacy by using a nickname unless that's the way they self-introduced

- Make sure that your pronunciation and spelling of their name is 100% accurate and spot on. This is a matter of respect.

Hello
my name is

Get It Right

Social Skill #9: AVOID BEING 'THAT' PERSON...

- ... the energy hog who takes all the air out of the room, creates nonstop drama, uses large elaborate gestures

- ... the one-sided conversationalist, who dominates the discussion and won't allow anyone else to get a word in

These two obnoxious types are really off-putting to all.

Social Skill #10: AVOID SHOWING DESPERATION

- Do not engage in clingy behavior, do not appear desperate for attention, for love, for anything – showing desperation is a real repellent

- Emotionally needy? High maintainence? Work on making those traits disappear

- Health issues? Personal problems?
Not good topics of conversation, even though 'misery loves company' and you would love to have other commiserators to share with, resist the urge to talk about your health issues or other problems socially.

The SmartyPants Secret on
SOCIAL SKILLS

Every person is wired to want to like, cooperate with, get along with other people; they are looking to connect with others – with you.

You just need to work on making them comfortable to be around YOU.

Good social skills can be developed, through first recognizing the problem areas, then finding alternate behavioral to counteract the problem, and then finally practicing new behavior.

BOOK BUYER BONUS

As a thank you to buyers, there is an additional free resource available only to book buyers. Did you get yours? If you missed it, go to www.SmartyPantsSecrets.com/bookbonus .

It's has additional valuable content and is free to book buyers, so don't miss out on getting yours!

BOOK RESOURCE

This SmartyPants Secrets book has a companion resource on the topic that may be of interest. The resource for this *Colors Book* is a personal best color determination for your unique personality.

If you would like to know what your **unique personality color** is, out of the 100s of available colors, visit the website at www.SmartyPantsSecrets.com/resources to learn more about how to get that special color that describes you best!

ABOUT

I am DR Martin, PhD* (*Personal human Development expertise) – Dolley Rapoport Martin. I took Dolley as my first name* in honor of the great First Lady Dolley Madison, whom I admire for her heroic actions in the White House during very turbulent times.

I took Rapoport as a middle name* in honor of Ingeborg Rapoport, who at age 103, is the oldest person to be awarded a Doctorate; finally getting the recognition due her from 77 years prior in Nazi Germany, unfairly denied her due to her Jewish roots. There is so much injustice in the world; it is an honor to recognize her achievement by taking her name. [*The selecting of one's name is an important exercise, since names are so personal and tied to identity. Yet most of us go through life with a name not of our choosing. Check out the SmartyPants Secret book NAMES.]

I have studied every communication subject for more than a decade, acquiring a large body of knowledge. I, perhaps like you, am a voracious reader and learner. My other strength is that I retain much of what I learn, so I can then compile the knowledge on a variety of subjects into a concise format, making the books that I author a shortcut on the best knowledge available. This saves you from going through all the data looking for the kernel that makes the greatest difference in success, the SmartyPants secret on a given topic.

I also have a mind that is ever curious about so many topics. I have earned multiple expert designations (education certified English teacher, Real Estate Broker, Stock Broker series 7, series 6, series, Certified Financial Manager, Insurance producer certified, Coach University) and held high level positions in business – large corporate entities, privately held companies, non-profit organizations, and startups – and have volunteered extensively, holding executive positions at the local, district and national levels. So I've been around the block more than once, on more than one topic.

Due to my research and experience, I have logged the perquisite time to carry the title of expert, giving myself an honorary PhD in the expertise area of communication, Personal human Development. I am passionate about sharing the knowledge that I have gained with you, in bite-size pieces.

And when a certain topic is not in my field of expertise, I find an expert with deep expertise in the field who has the knowledge that I seek. I then ask numerous in-depth questions of the expert to get to the gist, learn the SmartyPants Secret, to then pass the knowledge on in a book on the subject.

For other titles and additional resources, visit www.SmartyPantsSecrets.com

All book titles at www.amazon.com/-/e/B018HA35I8

Watch for content clips and helpful technique tips on a variety of topics coming soon at www.youtube.com/c/smartypantssecrets

Contact: Info@SmartyPantsSecrets.com